Travel In Stitches

Travel In Stitches

VOL.1

Laugh through your journey

Patrick Sam

This book was printed in the United States of America.

To order additional copies of this book, contact:
Xlibris Corporation
0-800-644-6988
www.xlibrispublishing.co.uk
Orders@xlibrispublishing.co.uk
301859

CONTENTS

DEDICATION

A compilation of everyday JOKES dedicated to travellers around the world hoping they arrive at their respective destinations with a smile on their faces.

Being happy does not mean everything is perfect. It means you have decided to see beyond the imperfections,

,,, Phil Kwashie's blog

Acknowledgements

I first of all give thanks to the Good Lord who gave me the strength and wisdom to make this day possible.

I am grateful to all my friends and family who inspired and supported me along the way. I share whatever achievement with you.

Life's best lessons are learnt in the most difficult of times.

. . . G. Chenwi's blog

Loads of love

Foreword

LAUGHTER IS THE MANIFESTATION OF JOY, AMUSEMENT OR MIRTH. IT IS AN AUDIBLE EXPRESSION OR THE APPEARANCE OF HAPPINESS OR AN INWARD FEELING OF JOY . . .

. . . according to the Oxford Advanced Dictionary.

There's a lot of searching going on these days for the elusive emotion of "being happy. Happiness allows us to think positive and consider many things in an optimistic way. It is the greatest feeling of satisfaction which is incomparable.

Simple, HAPPINESS is inside you. It's a kind of blissfulness that nobody can do except you.

1. **Throw out nonessential numbers like; age, weight and height. Let the Doctors, worry about them. That is why you pay them!**
2. **Make sure you keep only cheerful friends. The grouches pull you down.**
3. **No one is in charge of your happiness but You. Just make peace with your past so it doesn't screw your future.**
4. **Don't take yourself too seriously because no one else does. What other people think of you is none of your business**
5. **Try not to compare your life to others. You have no idea what their journey is all about. If we all threw our problems in a pile and saw everyone else's, we would grab ours back so quick.**
6. **The tears happen. Endure, grieve, and move on. The only person, who is with us our entire life, is ourselves. Be ALIVE while you are alive.**
    Life isn't tied with a bow, but it's still a gift.
7. **Cherish your health: If it is good preserve it, if it is unstable, improve it. If it is beyond what you can improve, get help.**

8. **Laugh often, long and loud. Laugh until you gasp for breath. Laughter is the only method used to exercise your facial muscles.**

    *Remember; laugh and everybody laughs with you,
    but snore and you sleep alone . . . . lol

Introduction

DO YOU REALISE; Today is the Tomorrow you worried about Yesterday?

The following is an old parable but it is one of those classics that could be read every day as a gentle reminder of the important things in your Life as you start a new day. Credit to Laura Bankston, author of Mayonnaise Jar and Coffee.

LIFE'S PHILOSOPHY

When things in your life seem almost too much to handle, when 24 hours in a day are not enough, remember the mayonnaise jar and the 2 cups of coffee.

A professor stood before his philosophy class and had some items in front of him. When the class began, he wordlessly picked up a very large and empty mayonnaise jar and proceeded to fill it with golf balls. He then asked the students if the jar was full. They agreed that it was.

The professor then picked up a box of pebbles and poured them into the jar He shook the jar lightly. The pebbles rolled into the open areas between the golf balls. He then asked the students again if the jar was full. They agreed it was.

The professor next picked up a box of sand and poured it into the jar. Of course, the sand filled up everything else. He asked once more if the jar was full. The students responded with an unanimous 'yes.'

The professor then produced two cups of coffee from under the table and poured the entire contents into the jar effectively filling the empty space between the sand. The students laughed.

'Now,' said the professor as the laughter subsided, 'I want you to recognize that this jar represents your life. The golf balls are the important things—your family, your children, your health, your friends and your favourite passions—and if everything else was lost and only they remained, your life would still be full.

The pebbles are the other things that matter like your job, your house and your car.

The sand is everything else—the small stuff. 'If you put the sand into the jar first,' he continued, 'there is no room for the pebbles or the golf balls. The same goes for life. If you spend all your time and energy on the small stuff you will never have room for the things that are important to you.

'Pay attention to the things that are critical to your happiness. Spend time with your children. Spend time with your parents. Visit with grandparents. Take time to get medical checkups. Take your spouse out to dinner. Play another 18. There will always be time to clean the house and fix the disposal. Take care of the golf balls first—the things that really matter. Set your priorities. The rest is just sand.'

One of the students raised her hand and inquired what the coffee represented. The professor smiled and said, 'I'm glad you asked.'

The coffee just shows you that no matter how full your life may seem, there's always room for a couple of cups of coffee with a friend . . .

The Prescription

A calm and respectable lady went into the pharmacy, right up to the pharmacist, looked straight into his eyes, and said,

"I would like to buy some hydrogen cyanide.

The pharmacist asked,
"Why in the world do you need hydrogen cyanide?"

The lady replied,
"I need it to poison my husband."

The pharmacist's was shocked and he exclaimed,

"Lord have mercy! I can't give you hydrogen cyanide to kill your husband! That's against the law! I'll lose my license! They'll throw both of us in jail! Absolutely not!

You **CANNOT** have any hydrogen cyanide!

The lady reached into her purse and pulled out a picture of her husband in bed with the pharmacist's wife.
The pharmacist looked at the picture carefully and replied,

"Well now. That's different. You didn't tell me you had a **PRESCRIPTION.**"

it's always important to read the small prints first

„Don't Mess with Grandma

In a trial, the prosecuting attorney called his first witness (an elderly woman) to the stand.

"Do you know me Mrs. Smith?" the attorney asked.

"Of course, I know you Mr. Collins since you were a boy and frankly, you've been a big disappointment to me. You lie, cheat on your wife, manipulate people and talk about them behind their backs. You think you're a big shot when you haven't the brains to realise you never will amount to anything more than a two-bit paper pusher. Yes, I know you".

The lawyer was stunned. Not knowing what next to do, he pointed across the room and asked Mrs. Smith yet another question;

"Do you know the defence attorney"? again, she replied;

"Of course, I've known Mr. Davids since he was a youngster too. he's lazy, bigoted, bulimic and has a drinking problem."

She continued "he can't build a normal relationship with anyone and his law practice is one of the worst in the entire state; not to mention, he cheated on his wife just like you, with three different women. Yes, I know him". the attorney was more than speechless. at this time, the judge brought the courtroom to silence, called both counsellors to his bench and in a very quiet voice, said . . .

"if either of you idiots asks her if she knows me, . . . i'll send you to the electric chair for contempt."

hmm! Seems everyone has skeletons in their cupboards

Why I Fired My Secretary

A month ago was my 50th birthday, I went to breakfast knowing my wife would be pleasant and say Happy Birthday, and would probably have a present for me.

She didn't even say Good Morning, Let alone Happy Birthday.

I thought, 'Well, that's wives for you. Maybe the children will remember?'

The children came in to breakfast and didn't say a word.

I went to the office feeling pretty low and despondent.

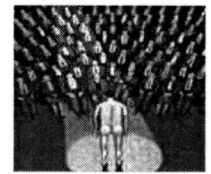

As I walked into my office, my secretary, Susan said, 'Good morning boss, Happy Birthday.'

So I felt a little better; at least someone remembers my birthday after all. Janet my secretary invited me to lunch to make my day.

We went out into the country to a little private place for lunch. On the way back to the office, she said,

'You know, it's such a beautiful day. We don't need to go back to the office, do we?'

I said, 'hmm no, I guess not' She said, 'Let's go to my apartment'
After arriving at her apartment she said, 'Boss, if you don't mind,

I'll go into the bedroom and slip into something more comfortable'

'Sure' I excitedly replied. She went into the bedroom and seizing the opportunity, I quickly stripped NAKED in wait.

In about six minutes, she came out carrying a big birthday cake, followed by my wife, children and dozens of our friends all singing Happy Birthday. and there on the couch I sat . . . NAKED. *Someone should give me a very good reason why i shouldn't fire her*

FatheR JosepH

skeletons in cupboards hm!

Be Careful What You Wish For

A man was sick and tired of going to work every day whiles his wife stayed home. He wanted her to see what he went through so he prayed:

'Dear Lord:

I go to work every day and put in 8 hours while my wife merely stays at home. I want her to know what I go through. So, please allow her body to switch with mine for a day. Amen!'

The good Lord granted the man's wish.

The next morning, sure enough, the man awoke as a woman. He arose, cooked breakfast for his partner, Awakened the kids, Set out their school clothes, Fed them, Packed their lunches, Drove them to school, Came home and picked up the dry cleaning, Took it to the cleaners And stopped at the bank to make a deposit, paid the bills and Went grocery shopping. Then, it was already 01 P.M.

And he hurried to make the beds, Do the laundry, vacuum, Dust, And sweep and mop the kitchen floor. He ran to the school to pick up the kids and got into an argument with them on the way home.

Set out milk and cookies and got the kids organized to do their homework whilst, he did the ironing.

At 4:30 he began peeling potatoes and washing vegetables for salad, breaded the pork chops and snapped fresh beans for supper.

After supper, He cleaned the kitchen, Ran the dishwasher, Folded laundry, Bathed the kids, And put them to bed and it was already 09 P.M.

He was exhausted and, though his daily chores weren't finished, he went to bed where he was expected to make love as well.

The next morning, he awoke and immediately knelt by the bed and said:—'Dear Lord, I don't know what I was thinking. I was so wrong to envy my wife's being able to stay home all day. Please, oh! Oh! Please, let us trade back. **Amen!'** The Lord, in his infinite wisdom, replied:

'My son, I feel you have learned your lesson and I will be happy to change things back to the way they were but the only problem is you'll have to wait nine months, though. **You got pregnant last night**.'

don't envy anyone

The Polish Remover

A polish man moved to the USA and married an American girl.

Although his English was far from perfect, they got along very well until one day he rushed into a lawyer's office and asked him if he could arrange a divorce for him . . .

The lawyer said that getting a divorce would depend on the circumstances, and asked him the following questions:

Lawyer: Have you any grounds?
Polish: Yes, an acre and a half and nice little home.
Lawyer: No, I mean what is the foundation of this case?
Polish: It made of concrete.
Lawyer: I don't think you understand. Is there a grudge?
Polish: No, we have a carport, and not need one.
Lawyer: I mean. What are your relations like?
Polish: All my relations still in Poland.
Lawyer: Is there any infidelity in your marriage?
Polish: We have hi-fidelity stereo and good DVD player.
Lawyer: Does your wife beat you up?
Polish: No, I always up before her.
Lawyer: Is your wife a nagger?
Polish: No, she's white
Lawyer: Hmm! Why do you want this divorce then?
Polish: She is going to kill me. I got proof . . .
Lawyer: What kind of proof?
Polish: She going to poison me. She buy bottle at drugstore. I can read and it say **'Polish Remover'**

Truly,,, he deserves a divorce

Mechanisms of the STOCK MARKET

Once upon a time in a village, a man appeared and announced to the villagers that he would buy monkeys for $10 each.

The villagers seeing that there were many monkeys around, went out to the forest, and started catching them. The man bought thousands at $10 and as supply started to diminish, the villagers stopped their effort.

He further announced that he would now buy at $20. This renewed the efforts of the villagers and they started Catching monkeys again.

Soon the supply diminished even further and people started going back to their farms. The offer increased to $25 each and the supply of monkeys became so little that it was an effort to even see a monkey, let alone catch it!

The man now announced that he would buy monkeys at $50.

However, since he had to go to the city on some business, his assistant would now buy on his behalf. In the absence of the man, the assistant told the villagers. "Look at all these monkeys in the big cage that the man has collected.

I will sell them to you at $35 each and when the man returns from the city, you can sell them to him for $50 each."

The villagers rounded up all their savings and bought all the monkeys.

Then they never saw the man nor his assistant again, only monkeys everywhere!

city workers huh!

Why I Gave Up on Baked Beans

One day I met a sweet gentleman and fell in love. When it became apparent that we would marry, I made the supreme sacrifice and gave up baked beans.

Some months later, on my BIRTHDAY, my car broke down on the way home from work. I called my husband and told him that I would be late because I had to walk home. On my way, I passed by a small diner and the odour of baked beans was more than I could stand. I figured that I would walk off any ill effects by the time I reached home, so I stopped at the diner and before I knew it, I had consumed three large orders of baked beans.

All the way home, I made sure that I released all the gas.

Upon my arrival, my husband exclaimed delightedly: 'Darling I have a surprise for dinner tonight.'

He then blindfolded me and led me to my chair at the dinner table. I took a seat and just as he was about to remove my blindfold, the telephone rang. He made me promise not to touch the blindfold until he returned and went to answer the call.

The baked beans I had consumed were still affecting me and the pressure was becoming most unbearable, so while my husband was out of the room I seized the opportunity, shifted my weight to one leg and let one go. It was not only loud, but it smelled like a fertilizer truck running over a skunk. I took my napkin from my lap and fanned the air around me vigorously still blindfolded.

Then, shifting to the other cheek, I ripped off three more. The stink was worse than cooked cabbage.

Keeping my ears carefully tuned to the conversation in the other room, I went on like this for another few minutes.

The pleasure was indescribable. When eventually the telephone farewells signalled the end of my freedom, I quickly fanned the air a few more times with my napkin, placed it on my lap and folded my hands back on it feeling very relieved and pleased with myself.

My face must have been the picture of innocence when my husband returned, apologizing for taking so long. He asked me if I had peeked through the blindfold, and I assured him I had not.

At this point, he removed the blindfold,  and twelve dinner guests seated around the table chorused: "Happy Birthday!'
I fainted . . . .

Simply Madness . . .

I visited a very rich friend and his polite maid came over to serve me; . . . .

maid: what would you like to have, fruit juice, soda, tea, chocolate, cappuccino, frapuccino or coffee?
Answer: Tea please.

maid: Ceylon tea, Indian tea, herbal tea, bush tea or honey bush tea?
Answer: herbal tea please, ,,, at least i can relate.

maid: how would you like it, black or white?
Answer: white

maid: ok, evaporated milk or fresh milk?
Answer: fresh milk will do please.

maid: goat's milk or cow's milk?
Answer: with cow's milk please

maid: freezeland cow or Afrikaner cow?
Answer: umm, i think I'll just take the black tea. Thank you.

maid: would you like it with sweetener, sugar or honey?
Answer: with sugar

maid: beet sugar or cane sugar?
Answer: cane sugar

maid: white, brown or yellow sugar?
Answer: on a second thought, i think i'll take a glass of water instead

maid: mineral water, tap water, distilled water or fizzy water?
Answer: mineral water will do, thank you.

maid: flavoured or non-flavoured?

Answer: forget it, and call me your boss and please don't ask me which, of them?

take your own drink whenever you visit the rich

If only Men understood the Meaning of,,,

(1) *Fine:* This is the word women use to end an argument when they are right and you need to shut up.

(2) *Five Minutes:* If she is getting dressed, this means a half an hour. Five minutes is only five minutes if you have just been given five more minutes to watch the game before helping around the house.

(3) *Nothing:* This is the calm before the storm. This means something, and you should be on your toes. Arguments that begin with nothing usually end in fine.

(4) *Go Ahead:* This is a dare, not permission. Don't Do It!

(5) *Loud Sigh:* This is actually a word, but is a non-verbal statement often misunderstood by men. A loud sigh means she thinks you are an idiot and wonders why she is wasting her time standing here and arguing with you about nothing. (Refer back to # 3 for the meaning of nothing.)

(6) *That's Okay:* This is one of the most dangerous statements a woman can make to a man. That's okay means she wants to think long and hard before deciding how and when you will pay for your mistake.

(7) *Thanks:* A woman is thanking you, do not question, or faint. Just, say you're welcome. (I want to add in a clause here—This is true, unless she says 'Thanks a lot'—that is PURE sarcasm and she is not thanking, you at all. DO NOT say 'you're welcome'; that will bring on a 'whatever').

(8) *Whatever:* Is a woman's way of saying sc*ew YOU!

(9) *Don't worry about it, I got it:* Another dangerous statement, meaning this is something that a woman has told a man to do, several times, but is now doing it herself. This will later result in a man, asking 'What's wrong?' For the woman's response refer to # 3.

*Get this right guyz and you'll be fine "hopefully"

I Wish I'll Never Grow Old

,,,,,Kids Stuff

OK, So we've taken off our clothes and I'm on top of you - how long before we get that orgasm thing?

I don't know but now I understand why mummy has a headache all the time!

Teacher asked: Which part of the body goes to heaven first?

A Kid replied: The legs . . . because every night I see my mum's legs up, high and screaming "OH GOD! I'M COMING".

TEACHER: Harold, what do you call a person who keeps on talking when People are no longer interested?

HAROLD : A Teacher.

TEACHER: Good, that's two hours detention for you.

* i love kids, they're innocent but so genuine*

Brilliant Kids . . .

TEACHER : Maria, go to the map and find North America.

MARIA : Here it is!

TEACHER : Correct. Now class, who discovered America?

CLASS : Maria!

TEACHER : Why are you late, Frank?

FRANK : Because of the sign.

TEACHER : What sign?

FRANK : The one that says, , , , , "School Ahead, Go Slow."

TEACHER : John, why are you doing your math multiplication on the floor?

JOHN : You told me to do it without using tables!

TEACHER : Donald, what is the chemical formula for water?

DONALD : H I J K L M N O!!

TEACHER : What are you talking about?

DONALD : Yesterday you said it's H to O!

TEACHER : Winnie, name one important thing we have today that we didn't have 10yrs ago

WINNIE : Me!

TEACHER : Can anybody give an example of COINCIDENCE?

TINO   : Sir, my Mother and Father got married on the same day, same time."

TEACHER : George Washington not only chopped down his father's cherry tree, but also, , , admitted doing it. Now, Tom, do you know why his father didn't punish him?

TOM   : Because George still had the axe in his hand.

TEACHER : Clyde, your composition on "My Dog" is exactly the same as your brother's. Did you copy his?

CLYDE   : No, teacher, it's the same dog!

The Guy with Family Problems

Two men met at a bus stop and struck up a conversation. One of them kept complaining of Family problems.

Finally, the other man got fed up and said: "You think you have family problems? Listen to my situation.

"A few years ago I met a young widow with a grown-up daughter and we got married.

Later my father married my stepdaughter. That made my stepdaughter my stepmother and my father became my stepson.

Also, my wife became mother in-law of her father-in-law. Then the daughter of my wife, my stepmother, had a son. This boy was my half-brother because he was my father's son, but he was also the son of my wife's daughter, which made him my wife's grandson. That made me the grandfather of my half-brother.

This was nothing until my wife and I had a son.

Now the half-sister of my son, my stepmother, is also the grandmother. This makes my father the brother-in-law of my child, whose stepsister is my father's wife, I'm my stepmother's brother-in-law, my wife is her own child's aunt, my son is my father's nephew and I'm My own grandfather!

And you think you have family problems HUH?

I'll love to measure this guy's stress level

Ooopsss!!!!

One day, a man came home and was greeted by his wife dressed in a very sexy lingerie. "Tie me up," she purred, "and you can do anything you want."

So He tied her up and went GOLFING.

....

A woman came home, screeching her car into the driveway, and ran into the house. She slammed the door and shouted at the top of her lungs, "Honey, pack your bags. **I won the lottery!**"

The husband said, "Oh my God! What should I pack, beach stuff or mountain stuff?"

"Doesn't matter," she said. "Just get out of the house." She shouted.

....

Marriage is a relationship in which one person is always right, and the other is a husband.

....

A Polish immigrant went to the DMV to apply for a driver's license.

First, of course, he had to take an eye sight test. The optician showed him a card with the letters:

'C Z W I X N O S T A C Z.'

"Can you read this?" the optician asked.

"Read it?" the Polish guy replied, "I know the guy."

....

A husband comes from church; he greets his wife and lifts her up. He carries her around the house.

The wife is so surprised and asks: "did the Priest preach about being romantic today"?

The husband said:

"No, he said we must carry our burdens and sorrows"

„,,The Smart Dog

A man hated his wife's dog so much that he decided to get rid of it.

He drove 20 blocks away and dropped the dog there.

The dog was already walking the driveway when he approached his home.

The next day, he decided to drop the dog forty blocks away, but the same thing happened. He kept on increasing the number of blocks but the dog kept on coming home before him.

At last, he decided to drive several miles away, turn right then turn left, past a bridge, then right again and another right and so on until he reached what he thought was a perfect spot and dropped the dog there.

"Now let's see how you get home" he muttered to himself.

Hours later, the man calls his wife at home and asks;

"Honey, is the dog there?"
"Yes, why do you ask"? wife replies:
Frustrated the man says, "Put that son of a b**ch on the phone, am terribly lost and need direction.

typical man: ask for directions mate.

The FBI Job

The FBI had an opening for an assassin.

After testing & checks there were 3 finalists;

Two MEN and a WOMAN . . .

For the final test, the FBI agents took one of the men to a large metal door and handed Him a gun.

'We must know that you will follow your Instructions no matter what the circumstances.

Inside the room you will find your wife sitting in a chair . . . . KILL HER!!'

The man said, 'You can't be serious. I could Never shoot my wife.'

The agent said, 'Then you're not the right man for this job. Take your wife and go home.'

The second man was given the same instructions. He took the gun and went, into the room. All was Quiet for about 5 minutes.

The man came out with tears in his eyes, 'I tried, But I can't kill my wife.'

The agent said, 'You don't Have what it takes. Take your wife, and go home.'

Finally, it was the woman's turn. She was given the Same instructions, to kill her husband.

She took the Gun and went into the room. Shots were heard, one

After another. They heard screaming, crashing, Banging on the walls. After a few minutes, all was Quiet.

The door opened slowly and there stood the

Woman, wiping the sweat from her brow.

'This gun is loaded with BLANKS' she said. I had to beat him to death with the chair.'

Hmm! That's the difference blokes

What a Husband

A blonde guy gets home early from work and hears strange noises coming from the bedroom. He rushes upstairs to find his wife naked on the bed, sweating and panting. "What's up?" he says.

"I'm having a heart attack," cries the woman.

He rushes downstairs to grab the phone, but just as he's dialling 999, his 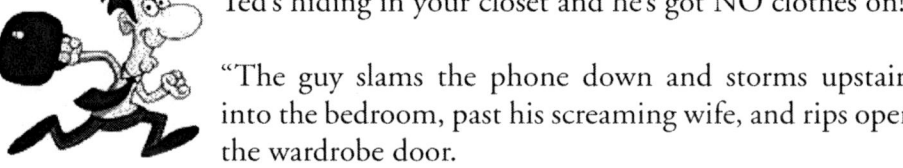 4-year-old son comes up and says; "Daddy! Daddy! Uncle Ted's hiding in your closet and he's got NO clothes on!

"The guy slams the phone down and storms upstairs into the bedroom, past his screaming wife, and rips open the wardrobe door.

Sure enough, there is his brother, totally naked, cowering on the closet floor.

"You rotten bastard," says the husband,

"My wife's having a heart attack and you're running around naked scaring the kids!"

*some men just can't read between the lines.

Don't Tempt Men

Bloke sat on a bus next to a beautiful lady. She starts breastfeeding her baby, but the baby won't feed so she says; "Come on, eat it all up or I'll give it to this nice man".

10 minutes later, baby is still not feeding so she says again; "Eat it all up or I'll give it to this nice man."

Bloke says; "Listen love, can you make up your flipping mind, I should have got off 4 stops away."

i wonder why men never get over breasts

Mistaken Identity

Tom and Mark were identical twins, who would confuse many people who did not know them.

Tom owned a dilapidated old boat, which sank the same day Mark's wife died.

A few days later, a kind old woman saw Tom and mistaking him for Mark, said,

 "I'm sorry to hear about your loss. You must just feel so terrible."

Tom, thinking that she was talking about his boat, replied;

"Heck no. In fact, I'm sort of glad to be rid of her. She was a rotten old thing right from the beginning. Her bottom was all shrivelled up and she smelled like old dead fish. She was always losing her water, and a bad crack in the back and a pretty big hole in the front too. Every time I used her, her hole got bigger and she leaked like crazy. I guess what finally finished her off was when I rented her to these four guys looking for a good time. I warned them that she wasn't very good, but they wanted to use her anyhow. The fools tried to get in her all at once and she split right up the middle."

The old lady fainted.

i think the gender for BOATS should be changed to masculine.

The Smart Lad,,,,

A young boy goes off to college, but about 1/3 of the way through the semester, he has foolishly squandered away all of the money his parents gave him. Then he gets an idea. He calls his daddy.

"Dad," he says, "you won't believe the wonders that modern education are coming up with! They actually have a program here at college that will teach our dog 'BRUNO' how to talk!"

"That's absolutely amazing," his father says. "How do I get him in that program?"

"Just send him down here with £1,000" the boy says. "I'll get him into the course." So, his father sends the dog and the £1,000.

About 2/3 way through the semester, the money runs out. The boy calls his father again. "So how's BRUNO doing, son," his father asks.

"Awesome, Dad, he's talking up a storm," he says, "but you just won't believe this—they've had such good results with this program that they've implemented a new one to teach the animals how to READ!"

"READ?" says his father, "No kidding! What do I have to do to get him in that program?"

Just send £2,500, I'll get him in the class." His father sends the money.

The boy now has a problem. At the end of the year, his father will find out that the dog can neither talk, nor read. So he SHOOTS the dog.

When he gets home at the end of the semester, his father is all excited.

"Where's BRUNO? I just can't wait to see him talk and read something!"

"Dad," the boy says, "I have some grim news. Yesterday morning, just before we left to drive home, 'BRUNO' was in the living room kicking back in the recliner, reading the morning paper, like he usually does. Then he turned to me and asked,

'So, is your daddy still messing around with that little redhead who lives on Downing Street?'

The father says, "I hope you SHOT that son of a b**ch before he talks to your Mother!" "I sure did, Dad!"

"That's my boy!"

Baptizing a Drunk

A man is stumbling through the woods totally drunk when he comes upon a Preacher baptizing people in the river.

The drunk walks into the water and subsequently bumps into the preacher.

The preacher turns around and is almost overcome by the smell of booze.

Whereupon he asks the drunk, "Are you ready to find Jesus?"

"Yes I am" replies the drunk, so the preacher grabs him and dunks him in the river.

He pulls him up and asks the drunk, "Brother have you found Jesus?"

The drunk replies, "No, I haven't." The preacher, shocked at the answer, dunks him into the water again, but for a bit longer this time.

He pulls him out of the water and asks again,

"Have you found Jesus, my brother?"

The drunk again answers, "No, I have not found Jesus."

By this time the preacher is at his wits end so he dunks the drunk in the water again, but this time he holds him down for about 30 seconds.

When the drunk begins kicking his arms and legs, the preacher pulls him up.

The preacher asks the drunk again, "For the love of God, have you found Jesus?"

The drunk wipes his eyes and catches his breath and says to the preacher,

"Are you sure this is where he fell in?"

what a way to deal with a hangover

Smart Leaders

Mandela is enjoying a hearty breakfast—bacon, eggs, coffee,croissants, toast, butter, jam, etc. when Bush, chewing gum, sits next to him and starts a conversation:

Bush: "You South Africans eat the whole bread?"

Mandela: "Of course."

Bush: (blowing bubble with his gum): "We don't. In the States, we only eat what's inside. The crusts we collect in a container, recycle, re-bake them into croissants and sell them to South Africa."

Mandela: "Oh Really?"

Bush: "Do you eat jam with the bread?"

Mandela: "Of course."

Bush: (chuckling and crackling his gum between his teeth): "We don't. In the States we eat fresh fruit for breakfast, put all the peels, seeds and left over's into containers, recycle them into jam and sell it to South Africa."

Mandela: "Do you have sex in America?"

Bush: "Of course we do."

Mandela: "And what do you do with the condoms?"

Bush: "Throw them away of course."

Mandela: "We don't. We pack them into containers, recycle them, melt them down into chewing gum and sell it to America."

Bush: (Beckoning grimacing to his secret service agents nearby): Get me Cheney and Rice on the line ASAP, get our Marines to stop South Africans from having sex ASAP.

at least i get my chewing gum from Ghana

,,,Men Under Attack

Q: What is the difference between men and puppies?
A: Puppies grow up.

Q: What do men have in common with ceramic tiles?
A: Fix them properly once and you can walk all over
them forever.

Q: If you drop a man and a brick out of a plane,
which one would hit the ground first?
A: Who cares????? . . . .

Q: What did God say after he created man?
A: I can do better than this! And then he created woman!!!.

Q: What's the difference between an intelligent man and a UFO?
A: I don't know, I've never seen either.

Q: What are two reasons why men don't mind their own business?
A: i) no mind ii) no business

Q: Why did Moses wander in the desert for 40 years?
A: Because even back then men wouldn't ask for directions.

Q: What is the difference between men and pigs?
A: Pigs don't turn into men when they drink . . .

Q: What makes men chase women they have no intention of marrying?
A: The same urge that makes dogs chase vehicles they have no
intention of driving.

Q: What do you do with a man who thinks he's God's gift?
A: Exchange him!!

Q: Why do men like smart women?
A: Opposites attract.

One day my housework-challenged husband decided to wash his sweatshirt. Seconds after he stepped into the laundry room, he shouted to me, "What setting do I use on the washing machine?" "It depends," I replied. "What does it say on your shirt?" He yelled back,

"Calvin Klein."

A couple is lying in bed. The man says, "I am going to make you the happiest woman in the world." The woman replies, "I'll miss you . . ."

"It's just too hot to wear clothes today," Jack says as he stepped out of the shower, "honey, what do you think the neighbours would think if I mowed the lawn like this?" "Probably that I married you for your money," she replied.

He said—Shall we try swapping positions tonight? She said— That's a good idea . . . you stand by the ironing board while I sit on the sofa and fart.

Q: What do you call an intelligent, good looking, sensitive man? A: A rumour!

GIVE UP MEN

Simple Logic

CALCULATIONS

Smart man + smart woman = romance
Smart man + dumb woman = affair
Dumb man + smart woman = marriage
Dumb man + dumb woman = pregnancy

OFFICE ARITHMETIC:

Smart boss + smart employee = profit
Smart boss + dumb employee = production
Dumb boss + smart employee = promotion
Dumb boss + dumb employee = overtime

SHOPPING MATH:

A man will pay #2 for a #1 item he needs.
A woman will pay #1 for a #2 item that she doesn't need.

GENERAL EQUATIONS & STATISTICS:

A woman worries about the future until she gets a husband.
A man never worries about the future until he gets a wife.
A successful man is one who makes more money than his wife can spend.
A successful woman is one who can find such a man.

HAPPINESS

To be happy with a man, you must understand him a lot and love him a little.
To be happy with a woman, you must love her a lot and not try
to understand her at all.

LONGEVITY:

Married men live longer than single men do,
but married men are a lot more willing to die.

PROPENSITY TO CHANGE:

A woman marries a man expecting he will change, but he doesn't.
A man marries a woman expecting that she won't change, and she does.

DISCUSSION TECHNIQUE:

A woman has the last word in any argument.
Anything a man says after that is the beginning of a new argument.

How I Stopped My Old Aunties Bugging Me!

Old aunts used to come up to me at Weddings, poking me in the ribs and cackling, telling me, **"You're next."**

They stopped after I started doing the same thing to them at Funerals.

For the Lads

CASE # 1

Interviewer to Millionaire:
To whom do you owe your success as a millionaire?
Millionaire: I owe everything to my wife.
Interviewer: Wow, she must be some woman.
What were you before you married her?
Millionaire: A billionaire.

CASE # 2

Wife: Why do you always carry my photo in your wallet?
Husband: When there is a problem, no matter how big,
I look at your photo and the problem disappears.
Wife: You see how miraculous and powerful I am for you?
Husband: Yes, I see your picture and say to myself,
"What other problem can be greater than this one?"

CASE # 3

Q—What is the difference between a mother and a wife?
A—One woman brings you into this world crying . . . .

. . . . the other ensures you continue to do so.

CASE # 4

Wife: Do you want dinner?
Husband: Sure, what are my choices?
Wife: Yes and No.

CASE # 5

Wife: Honey . . . . What are you looking for?
Husband: Nothing.
Wife: Nothing . . . ?? You have been reading our marriage certificate for an hour !!
Husband: I was just looking for the expiry date.

TIT for TAT

Wife comes home to find a note from husband;

My Dear Wife,

You will surely understand that I have certain needs that you with your 55-year-old body can no longer supply. However, I am very happy with you and I value you as a good wife. Therefore, after reading this letter, I hope that you will not wrongly interpret the fact I will be spending the evening with my 19-year-old secretary at the Lover's Inn Hotel. Please don't be perturbed, I shall be back home before midnight.

When the man came home, he found the following letter on the dining room table:

My Dear Husband,

I received your letter and thank you for your honesty. I would like to take this opportunity to remind you that you are also 55 years old. At the same time, I would like to inform you that while you are reading this, I will be at the Hotel Fiesta with Michael, my tennis coach, who, like your secretary is also 20. As a successful businessman, and with your excellent knowledge of maths, you will understand that we are in the same situation, although with one small difference: 20 goes into 55 a lot more times than 55 goes into 19.

Therefore, I will not be back until lunchtime tomorrow

The husband had heart attack

Guyz give up, women are just smarter.

World Economics Simplified

TRADITIONAL ECONOMICS
You have two cows
You sell one cow buy a bull
Your herd multiplies and economic grows
You retire on the income.

INDIAN ECONOMICS
You have two cows
You worship them.

PAKISTAN ECONOMICS
You don't have any cows.
You claim that the Indian cows belong to you.
You ask the US for financial aid,
British for warplanes,
Germany for technology,
Switzerland for loans,
Japan for equipment,
You buy the cows with all this
And claim exploitation by the world.

AMERICAN ECONOMICS
You have two cows.
You sell one; force the other to produce the milk of five cows.
You profess surprise when the cow drops dead.
You put the blame on some other nation with cows
You wage a war to save the world and grab the cows.

FRENCH ECONOMICS
You have two cows.
You go on strike because you want three cows.

GERMAN ECONOMICS
You have two cows.
You re-engineer them so that they live for 100 more years,
Only eat once a month and milk themselves.

BRITISH ECONOMICS
You have two cows.
They both have mad cow disease
You don't know what to do with them
You offer weak excuses

ITALIAN ECONOMICS
You have two cows.
You don't know where they are.
You break for lunch.

SWISS ECONOMICS
You have 2000 cows, none of which belong to you.
You charge others for storing them.

JAPANESE ECONOMICS
You have two cows.
You redesign them so that they are one-tenth the size of an
ordinary cow and produce twenty times the milk.
You create cute cartoon cow images called
'Cowkimon' & 'Cowagotchi'
You market them worldwide.

RUSSIAN ECONOMICS
You have two cows.
You count them and learn you have five cows.
You count them again and learn you have forty six cows.
You count them again and learn you have seventeen cows.
You give up counting and open another bottle of Vodka.

CHINESE ECONOMICS
You have two cows.
You get 300 people to milk them 24hrs a day.
You claim full employment, high bovine productivity
And arrest anyone reporting the actual numbers.
You then collect other people's cows to milk for a fee

NIGERIAN ECONOMICS
You have two cows.
You eat one and claim it was stolen
You call in the police to investigate and arrest everyone
living within 100km
Police torture them all, until someone admits kidnapping the cow
Police collects one cow each from all the people arrested
You have your cow back and the police now owns a cattle farm.

My Dad is the Most COWARD

Two kids are arguing over whose father is the most coward . . . .

The first one says," My dad is so scared that when a lightning strikes he slides underneath our bed."

The second kid goes," That's nuttin, my dad is so scared that when mummy works night shift he sleeps with the woman next door."

Oops,, "Too Late" Capt.

 The new Army Captain was assigned to inspect a company of soldiers in a remote post in the desert.

During his first inspection, he noticed a camel hitched up behind the mess tent.

He asks the First Sergeant why the camel is kept there.

"Well, sir," is the nervous reply, "as you know, there are 150 men here and no women. And sir, sometimes the men have . . . m-m-m . . . . urges. That's why we have the camel, Sir."

The Captain says, "I can't say that I condone this, but I understand about urges, so the camel can stay."

About a month later, the Captain starts having a real problem with his own urges. Crazy with passion, he asks the First Sergeant to bring the camel to his tent.

Putting a stool behind the camel, the Captain stands on it, pulls down his pants, and has wild, insane . . . m-m-m . . . . with the camel.

When he is done, he asks the First Sergeant, "Is that how the men do it?"

"Uhhhh . . . , No sir!" The First Sergeant replies. "We just ride the camel into town, where the girls are . . . !"

Blind Man Hits Back,,

Husband and wife are waiting at the bus stop with their nine children.

A blind man joins them after a few minutes. When the bus arrives, they find it overloaded and only the wife and the nine kids are able to fit onto the bus.

So the husband and the blind man decide to walk.

 After a while, the husband gets irritated by the ticking of the stick of the blind man as he taps it on the sidewalk, and says to him, "Why don't you put a piece of rubber at the end of your stick? That ticking sound is driving me crazy."

The blind man replies, "If you had put a rubber at the end of YOUR stick, we'd be riding the bus . . . so shut the hell up.

Prison v. Work

IN PRISON

you spend the majority of your time in an 8X10 cell.

AT WORK

you spend most of your time in a 6X8 cubicle.

IN PRISON

you get three meals a day (free).

AT WORK

you only get a break for one meal and you have to pay for it yourself.

IN PRISON

you get time off for good behavior.

AT WORK

you get rewarded for good behavior with more WORK.

IN PRISON

a guard locks and unlocks the doors for you.

AT WORK

you must carry around a security card and unlock open all the doors yourself.

IN PRISON

you can watch TV and play games.

AT WORK

you get fired for watching, TV and playing games.

IN PRISON

you get your own toilet.

AT WORK

you have to share.

IN PRISON

they allow your family, and friends
to visit.

IN PRISON

all expenses are paid by taxpayers
with no work at all.

AT WORK

you can not even, speak to your
family, and friends.

AT WORK

You pay all the expenses to go to,
work and then they deduct taxes,
from your salary to pay prisoners.

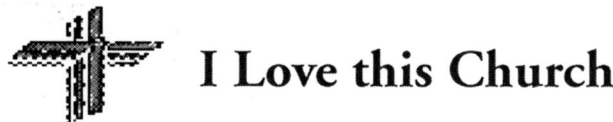 # I Love this Church

Preacher man says: "If I had all the beer in the world, I'd take it and throw it into the river". And the congregation cried, "Amen!"

"And if I had all the wine in the world, I'd take it and throw it in the river". And the congregation cried, "Amen!"

"And if I had all the whiskey and rum in the world, I'd take it all and throw it in the river". Again the congregation cried, "Amen!"

The preacher sat down. The deacon then stood up & said:

"For our closing hymn, let's turn to page 126 of our hymn books and sing, **'We shall drink from that river'"**.

THE CONGREGATION SCREAMED "HALLELUJAH"

Family Secrets

A young man went to his father one day to tell him that he wanted to get married. His father was happy for him. Cheerfully, he asked his son who the girl was, and the young man told him that it was Mary a girl from the neighbourhood. with a sad face the old man said to his son, "I'm sorry to say this son but I have to.

The girl you want to marry is your sister, but please don't tell your mother." The young man again brings three more names to his Dad, but ended up more frustrated because the response was still the same.

So he decided to go to his mother. "Mama I want to get married but all the girls that I love, dad said they are my sisters and I mustn't tell you."

His mother smiling said to him,
"Aah! Don't worry my son; you can marry any of those girls.

You're not his son anyway, but please don't tell your father."

comment reserved

She Asked for It!!!!

A couple have been married for 20 years. Every time they made love the husband insisted on switching off the light.

Well, after 20 years the wife felt this was ridiculous and decided to break the rule.

So one night, while in the middle of a wild, screaming, romantic session, she turned on the lights.

She looked down . . . and saw her husband holding a battery-operated pleasure device . . . a vibrator!

She went completely ballistic.

"You impotent bastard," She screamed at him, "how could you be lying to me all of these years? You better explain yourself!"

The husband looks her straight in the eyes and says calmly:

"I'll explain the VIBRATOR . . . you explain the KIDS."

The Doctor's Funeral

At the funeral of a **cardiologist,** his coffin was heart-shaped. A colleague doctor present started laughing which startled all the mourners.

When asked why he was laughing, he said. "I am thinking of the shape of my own coffin because I am a **gynaecologist**

am wondering what my will be like

#1 DAD

A daughter had not been to the house for over 5 years. Upon her return, her father angrily asked her:

"Where have you been all this time, you ingrate! Why didn't you write us, not even a line to let us know how you were doing? Why didn't you call?

You little tramp! Do you know what you've put your Mom through??!!"

The girl, crying: Sniff, sniff said . . . "Dad . . . I became a **prostitute . . .**"

"WHAT? Out of here, you shameless harlot, you're a disgrace to this family—I don't ever want to see you again!"

"OK, Dad—as you wish. I just came back to give Mom this fur coat and title to a mansion, a savings account certificate of £1 million for my little brother, and for you, Daddy, this gold Rolex, the spanking new BMW that's parked outside and a lifetime membership to the Country Club and and,,,

. . . an invitation for you all to spend New Years' Eve on board my new yacht in the Riviera, and . . . . just then the father stopped her and softly asked;

"Now what was it you said you had become sweetheart?"

Girl, crying again: Sniff, sniff "**A prostitute** Dad!" . . . Sniff, sniff

"Oh Gosh!—you scared me half to death, sweetheart!

I thought you said "a **Protestant**".

Come here and give your Daddy a hug!"

This guy deserves an OBE

Indescent Roposal

Johnny wanted to make love to a girl in his office . . . . but she belonged to someone else . . .

One day Johnny got so frustrated that he went up to her and said I'll give you a £100 if you let me make love to you . . . . but the girl said NO.

Johnny said I'll be fast, I'll throw the money on the floor, you bend down, and I'll be finished by the time you pick it up. She thought for a moment and said that she would have to consult her boyfriend . . . .

So she called her boyfriend and told him the story. Her boyfriend says ask him for £200, pick up the money very fast, he won't even be able to get his pants down. So she agrees and accepts the proposal.

Half an hour goes by and the boyfriend is waiting for his girlfriend to call.

Finally after 45mins the boyfriend calls and asks what happened . . . .

She said "The bastard used coins"!!

Always consider a business proposal in its entirety before agreeing to it.

A Lady's Prayer

Dear Lord,

I pray for Wisdom to understand my man;
Love to forgive him;
And Patience for his moods.
Because, Lord, if I pray for Strength,
I'll beat him to death . . . . AMEN.

„Men will Always be Men„„

 A man and his wife, now in their 70's, were celebrating their 50th wedding anniversary. On their special day a good fairy came to them and said that because they had been so good, each one of them could have one wish.

The wife wished for a trip around the world with her husband.

 Whoosh! Immediately she had airline/cruise tickets in her hands.

The man wished for a female companion 30 years younger . . . Whoosh . . . immediately he turned 100!!! *Gotta love that fairy!*

Visa Interview

An Arab was interviewed at the US Embassy for a Visa.

Consul: What is your name?
Arab: Abdul Aziz

Consul: Sex?
Arab: Six to ten times a week

Consul: I mean, male or female?
Arab: both male and female and sometimes even camels

Consul: Holy cow!
Arab: Yes, cows and dogs too!!!!

Consul: Man . . . . isn't it hostile?
Arab: Horse style, dog style, any style

Consul: Oh . . . . dear!
Arab: Deer? No deer, they run too fast!

*VISA REFUSED.

Spanish Lessons

A Spanish teacher was explaining to her class
that in Spanish, unlike English, nouns are
designated
as either masculine or feminine.
"House"
for instance, is feminine: **"la casa."**

"Pencil,"
however, is masculine: **"el lapiz."**

A student asked,
"What gender is 'computer'?"
Instead of giving the answer, the teacher split the class into
two groups, male and female, and
asked them to decide
for themselves whether
"computer"
should be
a **masculine** or a **feminine noun.**
Each group was asked to give four
reasons for its recommendation.

The men's group decided that
"computer"
should definitely be of the feminine gender
("la computadora"),
because:
1. No one but their creator understands their internal logic;
2. The native language they use to communicate with other computers is
incomprehensible to everyone else;
3. Even the smallest mistakes are stored in long term memory for possible
later retrieval; and
4. As soon as you make a commitment to one, you find yourself spending
half your pay check on accessories for it.

The women's group, however, concluded
that computers should be Masculine
("el computador"), because:

1. In order to do anything with them, you have to turn them on;

2. They have a lot of data but still can't think for themselves;

3. They are supposed to help you solve problems, but half the time
they ARE the problem; and

4. As soon as you commit to one, you realize that if you had waited a
little longer, you could have gotten a better model

*hmmm!!

Square Balls

An elderly woman walked into the Bank of England one morning with a bag full of money. She wanted to open a savings account and insisted on talking to the president of the Bank because, she said, she had a lot of money.

After many lengthy discussions and her persistence she was taken to the president's office.

The president of the Bank asked her how much she wanted to deposit. She placed her hand bag on his desk and replied, **£100,000***. The president was curious and asked her how she had been able to save so much money. The elderly woman replied that she made BETS.*

The president was surprised and asked, 'What kind of bets?'

The elderly woman replied, 'Well, I bet you £20,000 that you have square testicles.'

The president laughed out loud and told the woman that it was impossible to win a bet like that.

The woman never batted an eye. She just looked at the president and said, 'Would you like to take my bet?'

'Certainly', replied the president. 'I bet you £20,000 that my testicles are not square.'

'Done', the elderly woman answered. 'But given the amount of money involved, if you don't mind I would like to come back at 10 ' clock tomorrow morning with my lawyer as a witness.' 'No problem', said the president of the Bank confidently.

That night, the president became very nervous about the bet and spent the whole night in front of the mirror examining his testicles and confirming with his wife,,, checking them over and over again and reassuring himself that there was no way he could lose the bet.

The next morning at exactly 10 o'clock the elderly woman arrived at the president's office with her lawyer and acknowledged the £20,000 bet made the day before that the president's testicles were square.

The president confirmed that the bet was the same as the one made the day before. Then the elderly woman asked him to drop his pants etc. so that she and her lawyer could see clearly.

The president was happy to oblige.

 *To confirm the president's testicles were not square, the elderly woman examined the president's testicles in her hands with a little smile on her face.*

Suddenly the president noticed that the lawyer was banging his head against the wall. He asked the elderly woman why he was doing that and she replied, 'Oh, it's probably because I bet him £100,000 yesterday; that around 10 o'clock this morning I would be holding the balls of this Bank's President.

The Phone Call

A woman wanted to reach her husband on his mobile phone but discovered that she was out of credit, She instructed her son to use his phone to pass 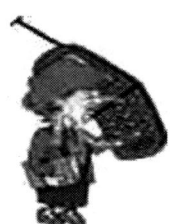 across an urgent message to his daddy who was on site. After junior had called, he got back to his mummy to inform her that there was a **lady** that picked up daddy's phone the three times he called his daddy.

She waited impatiently for her husband to return from work and upon seeing him in the driveway, she rushed out and gave him a slap, and she slapped him again, for good measure.

The neighbours rushed around to find out what the cause of the commotion was. The woman asked her son to tell everybody what the lady said to him when he called his daddy's phone.

Her son said "The subscriber you have dialled is not available at present. Please Try Again Later" . . .

She's facing divorce

Somebody's Raising Their Kid Right!

Teacher trying to explain **evolution** to a class asks pupil:

"Tommy do you see the tree outside?

TOMMY: Yes.

TEACHER: Tommy, do you see the grass outside?

TOMMY: Yes.

TEACHER: Go outside and look up and see if you can, see the sky.

TOMMY: Okay. (He returned a few minutes later) Yes, I saw the sky.

TEACHER: Did you see God up there?

TOMMY: No.

TEACHER: That's my point. We can't see God because he isn't there. Possibly, he just doesn't exist.

One of the pupils spoke up and wanted to ask TOMMY some questions. The teacher agreed:

PUPIL: Tommy, do you see the tree outside?

TOMMY: Yes.

PUPIL: Tommy do you see the grass outside?

TOMMY: Yessssss!

PUPIL: Did you see the sky?

TOMMY: Yessssss, now what?

PUPIL: Tommy, do you see the teacher?

TOMMY: Yes

PUPIL: Do you see her Brain?

TOMMY: No

PUPIL: Then according to what we were taught today in school, she possibly may, not even have one!

the pupil might be right

For the Ladies

For all those men who say, Why buy a cow when you can get milk for free. Here's an update for you:

Nowadays, 80% of women are against marriage, WHY? Because women realize it's not worth buying an entire pig just to get a little sausage. They claim:

Men are like . . . .

1. Men are like . . . **LAXATIVES . . . .** they irritate the crap out of you.
2. Men are like. **BANANAS** . . . the older they get, the less firm they are.
3. Men are like . . . **WEATHER** . . . Nothing can be done to change them.
4. Men are like **BLENDER** . . . you need One, but you're not quite sure why.
5. Men are like . . . **CHOCOLATE BARS** . . . . Sweet, smooth, & they usually, head right for your hips.
6. Men are like . . . **COMMERCIALS** . . . . You can't believe a word they say.
7. Men are like . . . **DEPARTMENT STORES**. Their clothes are always ½ off.
8. Men are like . . . **GOVERNMENT BONDS . . . .** they take so long to mature.
9. Men are like **MASCARA** . . . they usually run at the first sign of emotion
10. Men are like **POPCORN**. they satisfy you, but only for a little while.
11. Men are like **SNOWSTORMS** . . . you never know when they're coming, how many inches you'll get or how long it will last.
12. Men are like **LAVA LAMPS** . . . . Fun to look at, but not very bright.
13. Men are like **PARKING SPOTS** . . . All the good ones are taken, the rest, are handicapped.

awww, but you still love us gals

Politics Simplified

A little boy goes to his dad and asks, "What is **Politics**?"

Dad says, "Well son, let me try to explain it this way:

1. I'm the breadwinner of the family, so let's call me **CAPITALISM.**
2. Your mother is the administrator of the money, so we call her the **GOVERNMENT.**
3. We're here to take care of your needs, so we'll call you the **PEOPLE.**
4. The nanny, we'll consider her the **WORKING CLASS**.
5. And your baby brother, we'll call him the **FUTURE.**

"Now, think about that and see if it makes sense."

So, the little boy goes off to bed thinking about what Dad has said.

Later that night, he hears his baby brother crying, so he gets up to check on him. He finds that the baby has severely soiled his diaper.

So, the little boy goes to his parent's room and finds his mother sound asleep. Not wanting to wake her, he goes to the nanny's room.

Finding the door locked, he looks in the keyhole and finds his father in bed with the Nanny He gives up and goes back to bed.

The next morning, the little boy says to his father, "Dad, I think I understand the concept of politics now."

The father says, "Good, son, tell me in your own words what you think politics is all about"

The little boy replies,

"Well, while **CAPITALISM** is screwing the **WORKING CLASS**, the **GOVERNMENT** is asleep, the **PEOPLE** are being ignored and the **FUTURE** is in deep trouble."

bingo

By All Means . . . MARRY!

-*I recently read that love is entirely a matter of chemistry. That must be why my wife treats me like toxic waste.*

-**When a man steals your wife, there is no better revenge than to let him keep her.**

-*After marriage, husband and wife become two sides of a coin; they just can't face each other, but still they stay together*

-**By all means marry. If you get a good wife, you'll be happy. If you get a bad one, you'll become a philosopher.**

-*Women inspire us to great things, and prevent us from achieving them.*

-**I had some words with my wife, and she had some paragraphs with me.**

-*"Some people ask the secret of our long marriage. We take time to go to a restaurant two times a week. A little candlelight, dinner, soft music and dancing. She goes Tuesdays, i go Fridays."*

-**"I don't worry about terrorism. I was married for two years."**

-*"There's a way of transferring funds that is even faster than electronic banking. It's called MARRIAGE."*

-**"I've had bad luck with both my wives. The first one left me, and the second one didn't."**

-*Two secrets to keep your marriage brimming*

1. Whenever you're wrong, admit it,
2. Whenever you're right, shut up.

-The most effective way to remember your wife's birthday is to forget it once . . .

-My wife and I were happy for twenty years. Then we met.

-Marriage is the only war where one sleeps with the enemy.

-A son asked his Dad how much it costs to get married. His Dad replied: I don't know son, I'm still paying.

-A man inserted an 'ad' in the classifieds: "Wife wanted". Next day he received a hundred letters. They all said the same thing: "You can have mine."

We are ZULUS

An airplane is en-route to the United States. The pilot says:

'Ladies and Gentlemen, the plane is losing altitude and all the baggage must be thrown out.' So he did.

A little later, the pilot says:

'We're still losing altitude; we must throw anything out that is in the cabin'.

The plane continues its descent despite more things being thrown out.

Pilot: 'Still going down—we must throw out some people'. There's a big gasp from the passengers!

Pilot: 'Please don't panic;' to make this fair, passengers will be thrown out in alphabetical order. So i'll start from A to Z;

    a. any **Africans** on board?'
        but no one moves.
    b. any **Blacks** on board?'
        no one moves.
    c. any **Caribbean** on board?'
        Still, no one moves.

A little black boy—asks his dad:

Dad if we're neither **B**lacks nor **A**fricans . . . what are we then?

Dad says: "son, tonight we are Zulus!'

They got to their destination by the time the list got to Z

Confident Salesman

A new vacuum cleaner salesman knocked at door, a lady opened it. Before she could speak, the salesman rushed into the living room & emptied a bag of cow dung on the carpet: Ohh nooo! She screamed

Salesman:
"Madam, if I'm unable to clean up this dung with my new powerful vacuum cleaner in next 10 seconds, I'll EAT all this Crap"

Lady:
"Do you need Chilli Sauce with that s**t ?"

Salesman: "why?"

Lady:
"Because there's no electricity in the house"

The Pastor's Last Wish

An old pastor lay dying. He sent a message for the Head of Inland Revenue and his Lawyer to come to the hospital.

When they arrived, they were ushered up to his room. As they entered the room, the pastor held out his hands and motioned for them to sit on each side of the bed. The pastor grasped their hands, sighed contentedly, smiled, and stared at the ceiling. For a time, no one said anything.

Both the Inland Revenue Chief and the Lawyer were touched and flattered that the old man would ask them to be with him during his final moments. They were also puzzled because the pastor had never given any indication that he particularly liked either of them.

Finally, the Lawyer asked, 'Pastor, why did you ask the two of us to come here?'

The old pastor mustered all his strength, and then said weakly, 'Jesus died between two thieves, and that's how I'd like to go.'

should have called his MPs as well

Confession

A woman is having an affair during the day while her husband is at work.

Her nine-year-old son comes home unexpectedly, sees the illegal lover and hides in the bedroom cupboard to watch.

Then the woman's husband unexpectedly comes home.

She hides her lover in the cupboard, not realizing that her little boy is in there already.

The little Boy says: **"Dark in here."**

The Man says: **"Yes, it is."**

Boy: *"I have a soccer ball, do you want to buy it?"*

Man: **"No, thanks."**

Boy: *"My dad's outside, I'll call him if you don't buy it!"*

Man: **"OK, how much?"**

Boy: **"£100"**

A few weeks later it happened again and the boy and the lover were in the cupboard together again.

Boy: **"Dark in here."**

Man: **"Yes, it is."**

Boy: *"I have soccer boots."*

The Man, remembering the last time, asks the boy: "How much?"

The Boy says: **"£200"**

The Man says: **"Fine, I will buy them."**

A few days later, the Father says to the boy:

"Grab your ball and boots, *let's go outside and have a game."*

The Boy says: **"I can't, I sold them for £300"**

The Father says: "That's terrible to overcharge your friends like that . . . £300 is way more than those two things cost.

I'm going to take you to church and make you confess your **"SINS."**

They go to church and the father makes the little boy sit in the confession booth and he closes the door.

The Boy says: **"Dark in here."**

The Priest says: "Don't start that SHIT here!"

THIS IS MY CHURCH NOT YOUR FATHER'S HOUSE

hmm, comment reserved

The Vain Nigerian

A very successful Nigerian Man parked his brand-new Lexus in front of his office, ready to show it off to his colleagues. As he got out, a truck passed too close and completely tore off the door on the driver's side.

The man immediately grabbed his cell phone, called the cops, and within minutes a policeman pulled up. Before the officer had a chance to ask any questions, the Nigerian man started screaming hysterically. His Lexus, which he had just picked up the day before, was now completely ruined and would never be the same, no matter what the body shop did to it.

When the man finally calmed down from his ranting and raving, the officer shook his head in disgust and disbelief. "I can't believe how materialistic you Nigerians are" he said "You are so focused on your possessions that you don't notice anything else."

"How can you say such a thing?" asked the Nigerian man.

The cop replied, "Don't you know that your left arm's missing from the elbow down? It must have been torn off when the truck hit you."

"My God!" screamed the Nigerian. "Where's my Rolex?"

Speeding Hyms

If you MUST speed on the highway, sing these hymns loudly:

at **45 mph** . . . . "God Will Take Care of Me"

at **55 mph** . . . . "Guide me, O Great Jehovah"

at **65 mph** . . . . "Nearer My God to Thee"

at **75 mph** . . . . "Nearer Still Nearer"

at **85 mph** . . . . "This World is Not My Home"

at**95 mph** . . . . "Lord, I'm Coming Home"

at**100 mph** . . . . "Precious Memories"

Tit Bits

Man comes home, finds his wife with his friend in bed. He shoots his friend and kills him.

Wife says "If you behave like this, you will lose ALL your friends"

....

What is the definition of Mistress?

Someone between the Mister and Mattress

....

Husband tells wife, "Did u know the meaning of **WIFE** meant,,,

Without **I**nformation **F**ighting **E**verytime . . . !

Wife replies," No, It means, **WITH IDIOT FOR EVER!!!**"

....

What's the difference between Stress, Tension and Panic?

Stress is when wife is pregnant;

Tension is when girlfriend is pregnant and Panic is when both are pregnant.

....

Teacher asks kid: "Do you know the importance of a period?

Kid: "Yeah, once my sister said she has missed one, my Mom fainted, Dad got a heart attack & our Driver ran away.

. . . .

A woman asks a man who is travelling with six children, "Are all these kids yours??"

The man replies, "No, I work in a condom factory and they are Customer Complaints".

i was a victim as well

Life Sentence!

The bride tells her husband, "Honey, you know I'm a virgin and don't know anything about sex. Can you explain it to me first?"

"OK, sweetheart. Putting it simple, we will call your private place 'the prison' and my private thing 'the prisoner'. So what we do is: put the prisoner in the prison."

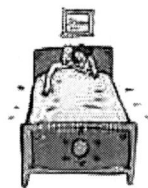 And then they made love for the first time. Afterwards, the guy is lying face up on the bed, smiling with satisfaction. Nudging him, the bride giggles, "Honey the prisoner has escaped."

Turning on his side, he smiles "Then all we have to do is re-imprison him."

After the second time they spent, the guy reaches for his cigarettes but the bride, thoroughly enjoying the new experience of making love, gives him a suggestive smile, "Honey, the prisoner escaped again!"

The man rises to the occasion, but with unsteady legs of a recently born foal. Afterwards he lays on his back totally exhausted.

She nudges him and says, "Honey, sorry to bother you, but the prisoner is out again."

Limply; turning his head, he YELLS at her, "Hey, it's not a life sentence, OKAY!!!" . . . .

What a way to start the day! Bet the prisoner is out on parole

Prophetic Daughter

 A father put his three year old daughter to Bed, told her a story listened to her prayer which she ended by saying: "God bless Mommy, God bless Daddy, God bless Grandma, and **good-bye Grandpa.**"

The father asked, "Why did you say **good-bye grandpa**?" The little girl said, "I don't know daddy, it just seemed like the thing to say."

The next day grandpa died. The father thought it was a strange coincidence. A few months later the father put the girl to bed and listened to her prayers which went like this: "God bless Mommy, God Bless Daddy and **Good-bye Grandma**." The next day the grandmother died.

"Oh my Gosh" thought the father, "this kid is in contact with the other side." Several weeks later when the girl was going to bed the dad heard her say: "God bless Mommy and **good-bye Daddy.**"

He practically went into shock. He couldn't sleep all night and got up at the crack of dawn to go to his office. He was nervous as a cat all day, had lunch sent in and watched the clock. He figured if he could get by until midnight he would be okay. He felt safe in the office, so instead of going home at the end of the day he stayed there, drinking coffee, looking at his watch and jumping at every sound. Finally midnight arrived; he breathed a sigh of relief and went home, he wasn't dead yet.

When he got home his wife asked, "I've never seen you work so late, what's the matter?" He said, "I don't want to talk about it, I've just spent the worst day of my life."

She replied, "You think you had a bad day, you'll never believe what happened to me.

This morning the **Gardener** dropped dead in our backyard while I was watching!"

DNA DNA please

Why Men are Never Depressed

Men Are Just Happier People—What do you expect from such simple **Creatures?**
Your last name stays put. The garage is all yours. Wedding plans take care of themselves. Chocolate is just another snack. You can be President. You can never be pregnant. You can wear a white T-shirt to a water park. You can wear NO shirt to a water park. Car mechanics tell you the truth.

The world is your urinal. You never have to drive to another petrol station toilet because this one is just too dirty, just stand at the door and aim!. You don't have to stop and think of which way to turn a nut on a bolt.

Same work, more pay. Wrinkles add character. Wedding dress £2000. Tux rental £50. People never stare at your chest when you're talking to them.

New shoes don't cut, blister, or mangle your feet. One mood all the time. Phone conversations are over in 30 seconds flat. You know stuff about trucks . . . A five-day vacation requires only one suitcase. You can open all your own jars. You get extra credit for the slightest act of thoughtfulness. If Someone forgets to invite you; he or she can still be your friend.

Your underwear is £2.50 for a three-pack. Three pairs of shoes are more than enough. You almost never have strap problems in public.

You are unable to see wrinkles in your clothes. Everything on your face stays its original colour. The same hairstyle lasts for years, maybe decades.

You can play with toys all your life. One wallet and one pair of shoes—one colour for all seasons. You can wear shorts no matter how your legs look. You can "do" your nails with a pocket knife. You have freedom of choice concerning growing a moustache.

You can do Christmas shopping for 25 relatives on December 24 in 25 minutes!

No wonder men are happier.

for sure

„„„„Real Courtroom Dramas

ATTORNEY: Now doctor, "isn't it true that when a person dies in his sleep, he doesn't know about it until the next morning?"
WITNESS: Did you actually pass the bar exam?

ATTORNEY: The youngest son, the twenty-year-old, how old is he?
WITNESS: He's twenty, much like your IQ.

ATTORNEY: Were you present when your picture was taken?
WITNESS: Are you shitting me?

ATTORNEY: So the date of conception (of the baby) was August 8th?
WITNESS: Yes.
ATTORNEY: And what were you doing at that time?
WITNESS: Getting laid

ATTORNEY: She had three children, right?
WITNESS: Yes.
ATTORNEY: How many were boys?
WITNESS: None.
ATTORNEY: Were there any girls?
WITNESS: Your Honour, I think I need a different attorney. Can I get a new attorney please?

ATTORNEY: How was your first marriage terminated?
WITNESS: By death.
ATTORNEY: And by whose death was it terminated?
WITNESS: Take a guess.

ATTORNEY: Can you describe the individual?
WITNESS: He was about 20, medium height, and had a beard.
ATTORNEY: Was this a male or a female?
WITNESS: Unless the Circus was in town I'm going with male.

ATTORNEY: Doctor, how many of your autopsies have you performed on dead people?

WITNESS: All of them. The live ones put up too much of a fight.

ATTORNEY: ALL your responses MUST be oral, OK?
What school did you go to?

WITNESS: Oral.

ATTORNEY: Do you recall the time that you examined the body?

WITNESS: The autopsy started around 8:30 p.m.

ATTORNEY: And, Mr. Denton was dead at the time?

WITNESS: If not, he was by the time I finished.

ATTORNEY: Are you qualified to give a urine sample?

WITNESS: Are you qualified to ask that question?

ATTORNEY: Doctor, before you performed the autopsy, did you, check for a pulse?

WITNESS: No.

ATTORNEY: Did you check for blood pressure?

WITNESS: No.

ATTORNEY: Did you check for breathing?

WITNESS: No.

ATTORNEY: So, then it is possible that the patient was alive when you began the autopsy?

WITNESS: No.

ATTORNEY: How can you be so sure, Doctor?

WITNESS: Because his brain was sitting on my desk in a jar.

ATTORNEY: I see, but could the patient have still been alive nevertheless?

WITNESS: Yes, it is possible that he could have been alive and practicing law. Nonsense!

ATTORNEY: *Are you sexually active?*

WITNESS: *No, I just lie there.*

ATTORNEY: *What gear were you in at the moment of the impact?*

WITNESS: *Gucci sweats and Reeboks.*

ATTORNEY: *This myasthenia gravis, does it affect your memory at all?*

WITNESS: Yes.
ATTORNEY: And in what ways does it affect your memory?
WITNESS: I forget.
ATTORNEY: You forget? Can you give us an example of something you, , , forgot?

ATTORNEY: What was the first thing your husband said to you that morning?
WITNESS: He said, 'Where am I, Cathy?'
ATTORNEY: And why did that upset you?
WITNESS: My name is Susan!

JUDGE: So, when did you realize that you were raped?
Prostitute: When the cheque bounced!

i admit we sometimes ask silly questions

Human Geography

GEOGRAPHY OF A WOMAN

Between 18 and 20
a woman is like Africa, half discovered, half wild,
naturally beautiful with fertile deltas.

Between 21 and 30
a woman is like America, well developed and open to
trade especially for someone with cash.

Between 31 and 35
she is like India, very hot, relaxed and convinced
of her own beauty.

Between 36 and 40
a woman is like France, Gently aging but still a
warm and desirable place to visit.

Between 41 and 50
she is like Yugoslavia, lost the war, haunted by past
mistakes. Massive reconstruction is now necessary.

Between 51 and 60
she is like Russia, very wide and borders are un-patrolled.
The frigid climate keeps people away.

Between 61 and 70
a woman is like Mongolia, with a glorious and
all conquering past.

After 70
they become Afghanistan. Almost everyone knows where
it is, but no one wants to go there.

THE GEOGRAPHY OF A MAN

Between 15 and 70
a man is like North Korea—ruled by one DICTATOR.

simple

„Wrong Number

Ring ring "Hi honey, this is Daddy . . . is your Mommy near the phone?"

"No Daddy, she's upstairs in the bedroom with Uncle Frank,"

After a brief pause Daddy says, "But you haven't got an Uncle Frank, honey!"

"Oh Yes I do, and he's upstairs in the bedroom with Mommy right now!"

"Uh Okay then . . . . here's what I want you do. Put down the phone, run upstairs and knock on the bedroom door and shout to Mommy and Uncle Frank that Daddy's car just pulled up outside the house."

"Okay Daddy!" A few minutes later the little girl comes back to the phone.

"Well I did what you said, Daddy."

"And what happened?" he asks.

"Well, Mommy got all scared, jumped out of bed with no clothes on and ran around screaming, then she tripped over the rug and went flying out the front window and now she's all bleeding with a broken neck."

"Oh my God!!!!! And what about your Uncle Frank?"

"He jumped out of bed with no clothes on too and he was all scared and he jumped out the back window into the swimming pool . . . . but he must have forgotten that last week you took out all the water to clean it, so he hit the bottom of the swimming pool and now he's writhing in pain"

*** Long pause ***

Then Daddy says, "Swimming pool???? Is this 555-7066?

"No! This is 555-7069" the little girl said.

"Ooops . . . . sorry wrong number!"

Ooops! THAT WAS CLOSE

Issues in Marriage!!!

A man took his wife to the rodeo and one of the first exhibits they stopped at was the breeding bulls. They went up to the first pen and there was a sign attached that said,

'THIS BULL MATED 50 TIMES LAST YEAR'

The wife playfully nudged her husband in the ribs and said, 'He mated 50 times last year.'

They walked to the second pen which had a sign attached that said,

"THIS BULL MATED 150 TIMES LAST YEAR'

The wife gave her husband a healthy jab and said, 'That's more than twice a week! You could learn a lot from him.'

They walked to the third pen and it had a sign attached that said, in capital letters,

'THIS BULL MATED 365 TIMES LAST YEAR'
The wife, so excited that her elbow nearly broke her husband's ribs and said, 'That's once a day. You could **REALLY** learn something from this one.

The husband looked at her and said, 'Go over and ask him if it was with the **same old miserable cow.**'?

*The husband's condition has been upgraded from critical to stable and he should eventually make a full recovery.

in every which way men lose

The Obedient Wife

There was a man who had worked all his life, had saved all of his money, and was a real "miser" when it came to his money.

Just before he died, he said to his wife . . . "When I die, I want you to take all my money and put it in the casket with me. I want to take my money to the afterlife with me."

 And so he got his wife to promise him, with all of her heart, that when he died, she would put all of the money into the casket with him.

Well, he died. He was stretched out in the casket, his wife was sitting there—dressed in black, and her friend was sitting next to her. When they finished the ceremony, and just before the undertakers got ready to close the casket, the wife said,

"Wait just a moment!"

She had a small metal box with her; she came over with the box and put it in the casket. Then the undertakers locked the casket down and they rolled it away. So her friend said,

"Girl, I know you were not fool enough to put all that money in there with your husband."

The loyal wife replied, "Listen, I'm a Christian; I cannot go back on my word. I promised him that I was going to put that money into the casket with him."

You mean to tell me you put that money in the casket with him!?!?!?"

"I sure did," said the wife. "I got it all together, put it into my account, and wrote him a cheque . . . . If he can cash it, then he can spend it."

women are just smart

The Genesis of Women's Problems

Ever noticed how all of women's problems start with **MEN**?
Woman has **Man** in it;
Mrs. has **Mr.** in it;
Female has **Male** in it;
She has **He** in it;
Madam has **Adam** in it;

Okay, Okay, it all makes sense now . . .
MENtal illness
MENstrual cramps
MENtal breakdown
MENopause
GUYnecologist
AND
When women have REAL trouble, it's a . . . **HIS**terectomy.
Hmmmmmmmm!!!!!!!

Men also have issues

Smart Thinking Pakistani Immigrant,,,

ASIF and HABIB are Pakistani beggars. They beg in different areas of London

HABIB begs just as long as ASIF but only collects £2 to £3 every day. ASIF brings home a suitcase FULL of £10 notes, drives a Mercedes, lives in a mortgage-free house and has a lot of money to spend.

HABIB says to ASIF 'I work just as long and hard as you do but how do you bring home a suitcase full of £10 notes every day?'

ASIF says, 'Look at your sign, What does it say'?

HABIB'S sign reads 'I have no work, but have a wife and 6 kids to support'.

ASIF says 'No wonder you only get £2-£3

HABIB says . . . 'So what does your sign say'?

ASIF'S shows his sign . . . .

It reads,

'I only need another **£10** to move back to **Pakistan**'

i'll keep asking for more demos just to be sure

Smartest Lad Ever

A first—std. teacher, Ms Smith was having trouble with one of her students.

The teacher asked, "Boy, what is your problem?"

Boy Answered, "I'm too smart for the first—std. My sister is in the third—std and I'm smarter than she is! I think I should be in the third—std. too!"

Ms Smith had enough. She took Boy to the principal's office.

While Boy waited in the outer office, the teacher explained to the principal what the situation was. The principal told Ms Smith he would give the boy a test to be sure.

Principal: What is 3x3?
Boy: 9.
Principal: What is 6x6?
Boy: 36.

And so it went with every question the principal thought a third-grade should know. The principal looks at Ms Smith and tells her, "I think Boy can go to the third-grade."

Ms Smith says to the principal, "I have some of my own question. Can I ask him?"

The principal and Boy both agree.

Ms Smith: What does a cow have four of that I have only two of?

Boy:	Legs.

Ms Smith:	What is in your pants that you have but I do not have?"
Boy:	Pockets.

Ms Smith:	What starts with a C and ends with a T, is hairy, oval, and delicious and, contains thin whitish liquid?
Boy:	Coconut

Ms Smith:	What goes in hard and pink then comes out soft and sticky?

The principal's eyes opened really wide and before he could stop the answer, Boy was taking charge.

Boy:	Bubblegum

Ms Smith:	Now I will ask some "Who am I" sort of questions, okay?
Boy:	Yep.

Ms Smith:	You stick your poles inside me. You tie me down to get me up. I get wet before you do.
Boy:	Tent
Ms Smith:	A finger goes in me. You fiddle with me when you're bored. The best, man always has me first.

The Principal was looking restless, a bit tense and took one large Patiala Vodka peg.

Boy:	Wedding Ring

Ms Smith:	I come in many sizes. When I'm not well, I drip. When you blow me, you feel good.
Boy:	Nose

Ms Smith:	I have a stiff shaft. My tip penetrates. I come with a quiver.
Boy:	Arrow

Ms Smith:	What word starts with a 'F' and ends in 'K' that means lot of heat & excitement?

Boy: Firetruck

Ms Smith: What word starts with a 'F' and ends in 'K' & if u don't get it
              u have to use your hand.
Boy: Fork

Ms Smith: What is it that all men have one of it's longer on some men
              than on others, the pope doesn't use his and a man gives it to
              his wife after they marry?
Boy: SURNAME

Ms Smith: What part of the man has no bone but has muscles, has lots of
              veins, like, pumping and is responsible for making love?
Boy: HEART.

The principal breathed a sigh of relief and said to the teacher,

The principal breathed a sigh of relief and said to the teacher,

"Send this Boy to the University, I got the last ten questions wrong myself!"

i recommend Harvard University

Genuine Kids' Concerns

These are original and genuine. No adult is this creative!!

JOE (age 3) was watching his Mom breast-feeding his new baby sister. After a while he asked: "Mom why have you got two? Is one for hot and one for cold milk?"

MEL (age 5) asked her Granny how old she was. Granny replied she was so old she didn't remember any more. Melanie said, "If you don't remember you must look in the back of your panties. Mine say five to six."

LEE (age 3) hugged and kissed his Mom good night. "I love you so much that when you die I'm going to bury you outside my bedroom window."

BRENDA (age 4) had an earache and wanted a pain killer. She tried in vain to take the lid off the bottle. Seeing her frustration, her Mom explained it was a child-proof cap and she'd have to open it for her. Eyes wide with wonder, the little girl asked: "How does it know it's me?"

SUE (age 4) was drinking juice when she got the hiccups. "Please don't give me this juice again," she said, "It makes my teeth cough."

DIRK (age 4) stepped onto the bathroom scale and asked: "How much do I cost?"

ROY (age 4) was engrossed in a young couple that were hugging and kissing in a restaurant. Without taking his eyes off them, he asked his dad: "Why is he whispering in her mouth?"

TONY (age 5) was in his bedroom looking worried. When his Mom asked what was troubling him, he replied, "I don't know what'll happen with this bed when I get married. How will my wife fit in?"

JOHN (age 4) was listening to a Bible story. His dad read: "The man named Lot was warned to take his wife and flee out of the city but his wife looked back and was turned to salt." Concerned, James asked: "What happened to the flea?"

PAM (age 4) was with her mother when they met an elderly, rather wrinkled woman her Mom knew. Tammy looked at her for a while and then asked, "Why doesn't your skin fit your face?"

so innocent, bless them

Some Old Men can Still Think Fast . . .

An elderly man in Texas had owned a large farm for several years. He had a large pond in the back. It was properly shaped for swimming, so he fixed it up nice with picnic tables, horseshoe courts, and some apple, and peach trees.

One evening the old farmer decided to go down to the pond, as he hadn't been there for a while and look it over.

He grabbed a bucket to bring back some fruit. As he neared the pond, he heard voices shouting and laughing with glee. As he came closer, he saw it was a bunch of young women—dipping in his pond naked. He made the women aware of his presence and they all went to the deep end.

One of the women shouted to him, 'we're not coming out until you leave, you old pervert!'

The old man frowned, 'I didn't come down here to watch you ladies swim naked or make you get out of the pond naked.'

Holding the bucket up he said,

'I'm here to feed the alligator.'

the guy should have taken a camera with him

Words

A husband read an article to his wife about how many
words women use a day . . .
30,000 to a man's 15,000.
The wife replied, "The reason has to be because we have to repeat
everything to men . . .
The husband then turned to his wife and asked, "What?"

Q: **What is the difference between men and women?**
A: **A woman wants one man to satisfy her every need.**
   A man wants every woman to satisfy his one need.

Q: **How do you keep your husband from reading your E-MAILS?**
A: **Rename the mail folder "Instruction Manuals**

The Pregnant Lady

A lady about 8 months pregnant got on a bus. She noticed the man opposite from her was smiling at her. She immediately moved to another seat. This time the smile turned into a grin, so she moved again. The man seemed more amused.

When on the fourth move, the man burst out laughing, she complained to the driver and he had the man arrested.

The case came up in court. The judge asked the man what he had to say for himself.

The man replied, "Well your Honour, it was like this, when the lady got on the bus, I couldn't help but notice her condition. She sat down under a sign that said, '**The Double Mint Twins are coming**' and I grinned.

Then she moved and sat under a sign that said, '**Logan's Liniment will reduce the swelling,**' and I had to smile.

Then she placed herself under a deodorant sign that said, "**William's Big Stick Did the Trick,**" and I could hardly contain myself.

But, Your Honour, when She moved the fourth time and sat under a sign that said, '**Goodyear Rubber** could have prevented this Accident' . . . I just lost it." "CASE DISMISSED!!"

Chocolate Peanuts

A tour bus driver is driving with a bus load of old seniors down a highway when he is tapped on his shoulder by a little old lady.

She offers him a handful of peanuts, which he gratefully munches up.

After about 15 minutes, she taps him on his shoulder again and she hands him another handful of peanuts.

She repeats this gesture about five more times whilst the bus driver kept munching them up.

When she is about to hand him another batch again he asks the little old lady, "why don't you eat the peanuts yourself?".

"We can't chew them because we've no teeth", she replied.

The puzzled driver asks, "Why do you buy them then?"

The old lady replied, "We just love the chocolate around them."

Heaven Clock

A man died and went to Heaven. As he stood in front of the Pearly Gates, he saw a huge wall of clocks behind him. He asked, "What are all those clocks?"

St. Peter answered, "Those are Lie-Clocks. Everyone on earth has a Lie-Clock. Every time you lie, the hands on your clock move."

"Oh", said the man. "Whose clock is that?"

"That's Mother Teresa's," replied St. Peter. "The hands have never moved, indicating that she never told a lie."

"Incredible," said the man. "And whose clock is that one?"

St. Peter responded, "That's Nelson Mandela's clock. The hands have moved twice, telling us that Mandela told only two lies in his entire life."

"Where's my Member of Parliament's clock?" asked the man.

"It's in my office. I'm using it as a ceiling fan!"

IT'S MOVING TOO FAST,,,, typical

What is Your OBSESSION?

A psychiatrist was conducting a group therapy session with four young mothers and their small children . . . 'You all have obsessions,' he observed.

To the first mother, Mary, he said: 'You are obsessed with eating. You've even named your daughter **Candy**.'

He turned to the second Mom, Ann: Your obsession is with money. Again, it manifests itself in your child's name**, Penny.**'

He turns to the third Mom, Joyce: 'Your obsession is alcohol. This too manifests itself in your child's name, **Brandy**.'

At this point, the fourth mother, Kathy, gets up, takes her little boy by the hand and whispers: 'Come on, **Dick**, we're leaving!

Extra Marital Affairs . . . .

The 1st Affair:

A married man was having an affair with his secretary.

 One day they went her place and made love all afternoon. Exhausted, they fell asleep and woke up at 8 PM.

The man hurriedly dressed and told his lover to take his shoes outside and rub them in the grass and dirt.

He put on his shoes and drove home.

"Where have you been?" his wife demanded.

"I can't lie to you," he replied, "I'm having an affair with my secretary. We had sex all afternoon."

"You lying bastard! You've been playing Golf!"

The 2nd Affair:

A middle-aged couple had two beautiful daughters but always talked about having a son.

They decided to try one last time for the son they always wanted.

The wife got pregnant and delivered a healthy baby boy.

The joyful father rushed to the nursery to see his new son.

He was horrified at the ugliest child he had ever seen.

He told his wife, "There's no way I can be the father of this baby. Look at the two beautiful daughters I fathered! Have you been fooling around behind my back?"

The wife smiled sweetly and replied, "Not this time honey!"

The 3rd Affair:

A woman was in bed with her lover when she heard her husband opening the front door.

"Hurry," she said, "stand in the corner."

She rubbed baby oil all over him, then dusted him with talcum powder.

"Don't move until I tell you," she said. "Pretend you're a statue."

"What's this?" the husband inquired as he entered the room.

"Oh it's a statue." she replied. "The Smith's bought one and I liked it so much I got one for us, too."

No more was said, not even when they went to bed.

Around 2 AM the husband got up, went to the kitchen and returned with a sandwich and a beer.

"Here," he said to the statue, "have this. I stood like that for two days at the Smith's and nobody offered me a damned thing."

The 4th Affair:

A man walked into a cafe, went to the bar and ordered a beer.

"Certainly, Sir, that'll be one cent."

"One Cent?" the man thought.

He glanced at the menu and asked, "How much for a nice juicy steak and a bottle of wine?"

"A nickel," the barman replied.

"A nickel?" exclaimed the man. "Where's the guy who owns this place?"

The bartender replied, "Upstairs, with my wife."

The man asked, "What's he doing upstairs with your wife?"

The bartender replied,

"The same thing I'm doing to his business down here."

The 5th Affair:

Jake was dying. His wife sat at the bedside.

He looked up and said weakly, "I have something I must confess."

"There's no need to," his wife replied.

"No," he insisted, "I want to die in peace. I slept with your sister, your best friend, her best friend, and your mother!"

"I know, I know," she replied. "Now just rest and let the poison work."

Unlucky Wish

A man walks into a restaurant with a full-grown Ostrich behind him. The waitress asks them for their orders.

The man says, 'A hamburger, fries and a coke,' and turns to the ostrich, 'What's yours?'

"I'll have the same,' says the ostrich".

A short time later the waitress returns with the order 'That will be £9.40 pleases. The man reaches into his pocket and takes out the exact change for payment.

The next day, the man and the ostrich come again and the man says, "A hamburger, fries and a coke."

The ostrich says, "I'll have the same." Again the man reaches into his pocket and pays with exact change.

This becomes routine until the waitress not being able to hold back her curiosity any longer asks:

"Excuse me, sir."*

"How do you manage to always come up with the exact change in your pocket every time?"

"Well," says the man, "several years ago I was cleaning my attic and found an old lamp. When I rubbed it, a Genie appeared and offered me two wishes".

My first wish was that if I ever had to pay for anything, I would just put my hand in my pocket and the right amount of money would always be there."

"That's brilliant!' says the waitress. 'Most people would ask for a million dollars or something, but you'll always be as rich as you want for as long as you live."

"That's right. Whether it's a gallon of milk or a Rolls Royce, the exact money is always there,' says the man".

The waitress asks, "What's with the ostrich?"

The man sighs, pauses and answers, **"My second wish was for a FIT BIRD with a big ass and long legs who agrees with everything I say."**

well you got yourself the fittest bird then mate

Modern Technology

THREE WOMEN, TWO YOUNGER, AND ONE SENIOR CITIZEN WERE SITTING NAKED IN A SAUNA.

SUDDENLY THERE WAS A BEEPING SOUND.
THE YOUNG WOMAN PRESSED HER **FOREARM** AND THE BEEP STOPPED.
THE OTHERS LOOKED AT HER QUESTIONINGLY.

"THAT WAS MY PAGER, SHE SAID.
I HAVE A MICROCHIP UNDER THE SKIN OF MY ARM."

A FEW MINUTES LATER, A PHONE RANG.
THE SECOND YOUNG WOMAN LIFTED HER PALM TO HER EAR.
WHEN SHE FINISHED, SHE EXPLAINED,

"THAT WAS MY MOBILE PHONE; I HAVE A MICROCHIP IN MY HAND."

THE OLDER WOMAN FELT VERY LOW-TECH.
NOT TO BE OUT DONE, SHE DECIDED SHE HAD TO DO SOMETHING JUST AS IMPRESSIVE.

SHE STEPPED OUT OF THE SAUNA AND WENT TO THE BATHROOM.

SHE RETURNED WITH A PIECE OF TOILET PAPER HANGING FROM HER REAR END.

THE OTHERS RAISED THEIR EYEBROWS AND STARED AT HER.

THE OLDER WOMAN FINALLY SAID . . . .
"WELL, I'M RECEIVING A **FAX**! . . . . Technology huh!

smashing! Old and wise

112

The Pensioner's New Hat

An old lady was standing at the railing of the cruise ship holding her hat tight so that it would not blow away in the wind. A gentleman approached her and said,

"Pardon me, madam. I do not intend to be forward but did you know that your dress is blowing up in this high wind?" "Yes, I know," said the lady. "I need both my hands to hold onto this hat."

"But madam, you must know that you are not wearing any panties and your privates are exposed!" said the gentleman.

The woman looked straight into the gentleman's eyes and replied,

"Sir, anything you see down there is 85 years old.

I just bought this hat yesterday!"

* mind your business mate*

Wife vs Husband

A couple drove down a country road for several miles, not saying a word.
An earlier discussion had led to an argument and neither of them
wanted to concede their position.
As they passed a barnyard of mules, goats, and pigs,
the husband asked sarcastically, "Relatives of yours?"
"Yep," the wife replied, "in-laws."

Don't dare them

Interesting Mix-Ups

DORMITORY:
When you rearrange the letters:
DIRTY ROOM

PRESBYTERIAN:
When you rearrange the letters:
BEST IN PRAYER

ASTRONOMER:
When you rearrange the letters:
MOON STARER

THE EYES:
When you rearrange the letters:
THEY SEE

GEORGE BUSH:
When you rearrange the letters:
HE BUGS GORE

SLOT MACHINES:
When you rearrange the letters:
CASH LOST IN ME

ELECTION RESULTS:
When you rearrange the letters:
LIES—LET'S RECOUNT

SNOOZE ALARMS:
When you rearrange the letters:
ALAS! NO MORE Z 'S

A THE EARTHQUAKES:
When you rearrange the letters:
THAT QUEER SHAKE

ELEVEN PLUS TWO:
When you rearrange the letters:
TWELVE PLUS ONE

AND FOR THE GRAND FINALE:

MOTHER-IN-LAW:
When you rearrange the letters:
WOMAN HITLER

The Innocent Calf

A man was heading home after binge drinking. On his way home, he was robbed by thieves. For not having much money on him, the gangs stripped him naked and took away his designer gear including his underwear.

They tied him to a tree completely naked and left him.

In the morning his worried wife woke up only to see her husband naked and tied to a tree. Very confused, she screamed until all the villagers came round.

They immediately untied and freed him. He immediately grabbed a stick went straight for a young calf which was grazing and started chasing it all over the compound.

When questioned, he said

"you have no idea what this calf has done to me the whole night!!!"

The calf had mistaken his manhood for the mother's tits and tried to suckle milk the whole night without success.

i bet he gained an inch extra

The Proud Daddy

A man has six children and is very proud of his achievement. He is so proud of himself, that he starts calling his wife,

"Mother of Six" in spite of her objections.

One night, they go to a party. The man decides that it's time to go home and wants to find out if his wife is ready to leave as well. He shouts at the top of his voice,
"Shall we go home 'Mother of Six?'

His wife, irritated by her husband's lack of discretion, shouts right back,
"Anytime you're ready, Father of Four."

hmm!

LIfe can be Tough When You're Stupid.
(True Stories)

—Recently, when I went to McDonald's I saw on the menu that you could have an order of 6, 9 or 12 Chicken Nuggets.

I asked for a half dozen nuggets.

'We don't have half dozen nuggets,' said the teenager at the counter.

'You don't?' I replied.

'We only have six, nine, or twelve,' was the reply.

'So I can't order a half dozen nuggets, but I can order six?'

'That's right.'

So I shook my head and ordered six Nuggets

(Unbelievable . . .)

—I was checking out at the local Tescos with just a few items and the lady behind me put her things on the belt close to mine. I picked up one of those 'dividers' that they keep by the cash register and placed it between our things so they wouldn't get mixed.

After the girl had scanned all of my items, she picked up the 'divider', looking it all over for the bar code so she could scan it.

Not finding the bar code, she said to me, 'Do you know how much this is?'

I said to her 'I've changed my mind; I don't think I'll buy that today.'

She said 'OK,' and I paid her for the things and left.

She had no clue to what had just happened.

-A woman at work was seen putting a credit card into her floppy drive and pulling it out very quickly.

When I inquired as to what she was doing, she said she was shopping on the Internet and they kept asking for a credit card number, so she was using the ATM 'thingy.'

(hmm!!)

-I recently saw a distraught young lady weeping beside her car. 'Do you need some help?' I asked.

She replied, 'I knew I should have replaced the battery to this remote door unlocker. Now I can't get into my car. Do you think they (pointing to a distant convenience store) would have a battery to fit this?'

'Hmmm, I don't know. Do you have an alarm, too?' I asked.

'No, just this remote thingy,' she answered, handing the car keys to me. As I took the key and manually unlocked the door, I replied, 'Why don't you drive over there and check about the batteries. It's a long walk . . . .'

—Several years ago, we had an Intern who was none too swift. One day she was typing and turned to a secretary and said, 'I'm almost out of typing paper. What do I do?' 'Just use paper from the photocopier', the secretary told her. With that, the intern took her last remaining blank piece of paper, put it on the photocopier and proceeded to make five 'blank' copies.

(huh!!)

-A mother calls 911 very worried asking the dispatcher if she needs to take her kid to the emergency room, the kid had eaten ants. The dispatcher tells her to give the kid some Benadryl and he should be fine, the mother says, 'I just gave him some ant killer . . . .'

Dispatcher: 'Rush him in to emergency!'

FINALLY; Something Mind Boggling

3 MEN GO INTO A HOTEL. THE MAN BEHIND THE DESK SAID THE ROOM IS $30, SO EACH MAN PAID $10 AND WENT TO THE ROOM.

A WHILE LATER THE MAN BEHIND THE DESK REALIZED THE ROOM WAS ONLY $25, SO HE SENT THE BELLBOY TO THE 3 GUYS' ROOM WITH $5 CHANGE.

ON THE WAY, THE BELLBOY COULDN'T FIGURE OUT HOW TO SPLIT $5 EVENLY BETWEEN 3 MEN, SO HE GAVE EACH MAN A $1 AND KEPT THE OTHER $2 FOR HIMSELF.

THIS MEANT THAT THE 3 MEN EACH PAID $9 FOR THE ROOM, WHICH IS A TOTAL OF $27, ADD THE $2 THAT THE BELLBOY KEPT = $29.

WHERE IS THE OTHER DOLLAR?

I've got it

Lightning Source UK Ltd.
Milton Keynes UK
172707UK00002B/2/P